THE ULTIMATE REPTILE FIELD GUIDE

THE ULTIMATE

REPTILE

FIELD GUIDE

APPLESAUCE
· PRESS ·

MY FIELD NOTES

A good field guide is a reptile lover's best friend. Field guides tell you everything you need to identify animals you see in the wild. How big is it? What color is it? Where can you find it? When you encounter a new reptile, you can consult your trusty field guide to know exactly what species it is. Everyone can use a field guide—from scientists who study reptiles (they're called herpetologists) to nature lovers.

There are a few things you can look for when hunting for reptiles in the wild. Reptiles are cold-blooded vertebrates, which means they have a spine, and they have dry skin with bony plates or scales. That skin sheds and regrows throughout the reptile's life.

Reptiles have been on Earth for more than 300 million years! Some common groups of reptiles you might recognize are turtles, crocodiles, lizards, snakes, and dinosaurs. Most reptiles have four legs, with the exception of snakes (and even though snakes don't have legs now, their ancient ancestors did). Their legs are usually short, and their bodies are often low to the ground.

Reptiles can come in all shapes and sizes, from a few inches long to 20 feet long. A lot of reptiles will have colors that match their surroundings, like brown and green, but they can also have bright shades, from pink to red to yellow and more. Reptiles have tails, and some will be short and thick, while others are long and curly. Many reptiles lay soft-shelled eggs, but there are some that give birth to live young.

As scientists study more and more species, they add notes to their field guides. Our understanding of a species grows every time we study a new animal. That can help scientists in understanding how different species are related to one another, and how their ancestors evolved. And knowing more about where a species lives and how it survives means that we can help keep it from going extinct. So as you see and research new reptiles, be sure to keep your own field notes. There's always more to learn!

LEATHERY
TEXTURED SHELL

WEIGHS 50 POUNDS
(23 KILOGRAMS)

GRAY- OR OLIVE-
COLORED SHELL

MALES HAVE
LONGER TAILS
THAN FEMALES

PADDLE-LIKE FLIPPERS

Its limbs aren't great for
walking on land, so this
freshwater turtle lives in the
rivers, ponds, and creeks of
Australia and New Guinea.

PIG-NOSED TURTLE
(CARETTOCHELYS INSCULPTA)

Lives in Australia
and New Guinea

**LONG, FLESHY SNOUT
THAT LOOKS LIKE
A PIG'S NOSE**

The pig-nosed turtle eats
mollusks and insects, along
with fruit, leaves, and flowers.

**CREAM, WHITE, OR
YELLOWISH COLORING
ON BOTTOM OF BODY**

**1.6–2 FEET LONG
(0.5–0.6 METER LONG)**

RED EYES

BLUNT HEAD WITH REAR FANGS

WEIGHS 6–7 POUNDS (2.7–3.2 KILOGRAMS)

SCENT GLANDS NEAR TAIL
When it feels threatened, the water snake releases a foul-smelling musk to deter predators.

3 FEET LONG (0.9 METER)

BOCOURT'S WATER SNAKE
(SUBSESSOR BOCOURTI)

Lives in Southeast Asia

BROWN BODY WITH
BLACK MARKINGS

SMOOTH SCALES

The Bocourt's water snake likes still water,
including swamps, ponds, and shallow
lakes. It stays close to the water during
the day to hunt for frogs and fish, and it
travels on land during rainy nights.

GALÁPAGOS PINK LAND IGUANA
(CONOLOPHUS MARTHAE)

Lives in the Galápagos Islands

PINK SKIN WITH DARKER PINK VERTICAL MARKINGS ⟶

The Galápagos pink land iguana is related to other land iguanas, but the pink iguana was officially classified as its own species in 2009 because its pink color is so unique. It's only found on Isabela Island, on the northern part of the island near the active volcano Vólcan Wolf.

MALES 4 FEET LONG (1.2 METERS); FEMALES 2–3 FEET LONG (0.6–0.9 METER)

SPINY RIDGE
DOWN THE BACK

SQUAT BODY WITH LEGS
SPRAWLING OUT TO SIDE

Land iguanas haven't adapted to spend
time in the water like other marine
iguanas. The pink land iguana is trapped
on the island where it lives, since it can't
swim, and the young iguanas are small
enough to be prey for feral cats and
rats on the island. There are fewer
than 200 pink land iguanas left.

TOE PADS

Geckos have tiny, microscopic hairs on their toe pads that allow them to climb easily. They grip so well that geckos can even stick to glass.

FLAPS ON SIDE OF BODY

The flaps allow the common flying gecko to glide through the air like a parachute.

WEBBED FEET

COMMON FLYING GECKO
(PTYCHOZOON KUHLI)

Lives in Southeast Asia

BROWN COLORING WITH MARKINGS

Its coloring looks like tree bark, allowing the common flying gecko to stay camouflaged during the day while it sleeps on tree trunks. Common flying geckos have more skin pigment than other nocturnal species, helping protect them from UV rays while they sleep.

**4–7 INCHES LONG
(10.2–17.8 CENTIMETERS)**

LEATHERBACK SEA TURTLE
(DERMOCHELYS CORIACEA)

LARGE FLIPPERS

The flippers are good for traveling long distances. Leatherbacks migrate between breeding and feeding areas, and their travels can take them up to 10,000 miles (16,093 kilometers) per year.

POINTED, TOOTHLIKE CUSPS AND SHARP-EDGED JAWS →

← 5-6 FEET LONG (1.5-1.8 METERS) →

Lives in the Atlantic Ocean, Pacific Ocean,
Indian Ocean, and Mediterranean Sea

FLEXIBLE, LEATHERY SHELL

It is the only species of sea
turtle without a hard shell. The
leatherback keeps itself warmer than
the water thanks to a layer of fat
and a unique blood vessel structure
that helps it retain heat better
than other cold-blooded reptiles.

THE LARGEST TURTLE IN THE WORLD

It weighs more than 1,000
pounds (454 kilograms).

STRONG SWIMMER

The leatherback sea turtle can dive much
deeper than any other turtle (and deeper than
most other ocean animals), going as far down
as 4,000 feet (1,220 meters), and it can hold its
breath underwater for up to 85 minutes.

BORNEO EARLESS MONITOR

(LANTHANOTUS BORNEENSIS)

Lives in Borneo

POWERFUL JAWS

It can swallow its prey underwater. It'll stand completely motionless underwater, waiting for fish and crustaceans to swim by that it can hunt.

THICK TAIL

The earless monitor has a prehensile tail, which means it can wrap around stones and branches. When it's in the water, this helps it to hold on during powerful currents without being swept away.

LONG NECK

The Borneo earless monitor is semiaquatic, which means it spends part of its time on land and part of its time in the water. The long neck helps the monitor lift its nose up to breathe when it's in the water.

POWERFUL LIMBS AND CLAWS

It is nocturnal, and during the day it digs a burrow to sleep in. While it's swimming, the strong limbs help it with quick spurts of speed.

1–2 FEET LONG (0.3–0.6 METER)

YELLOW-BELLIED SEA SNAKE

(HYDROPHIS PLATURUS)

LONG SNOUT

VENOMOUS FRONT FANGS

PADDLE-LIKE TAIL FOR SWIMMING

It can dive dozens of feet down into the water and even swim backward, but sometimes it just floats along with the ocean currents. This sea snake isn't well suited to spend any time on land.

3 FEET LONG (0.9 METER)

Lives in the Indian Ocean
and Pacific Ocean

BROWN BACK

The yellow-bellied sea snake has a
unique method of breathing, pulling
in oxygen from the water through its
skin. It lives in warm, shallow saltwater
and can stay under the surface for
hours without coming up for air.

UNDERSIDE OF BODY
HAS A VIBRANT,
YELLOW STRIPE

GLAND IN NOSE THAT FILTERS OUT SALT

This iguana needs to spend time both in the ocean and on land. It sleeps along the coastline or in mangrove trees and lays its eggs on sandy beaches. When it's in the water, the special glands filter out the extra salt like a sneeze.

TRICUSPID (3-TIPPED) TEETH

The Christmas marine iguana feeds on algae that grow in the water. The water where it feeds is cold, so it needs to spend a lot of time sunbathing to warm itself up again.

CHRISTMAS MARINE IGUANA
(AMBLYRHYNCHUS CRISTATUS VENUSTISSIMUS)

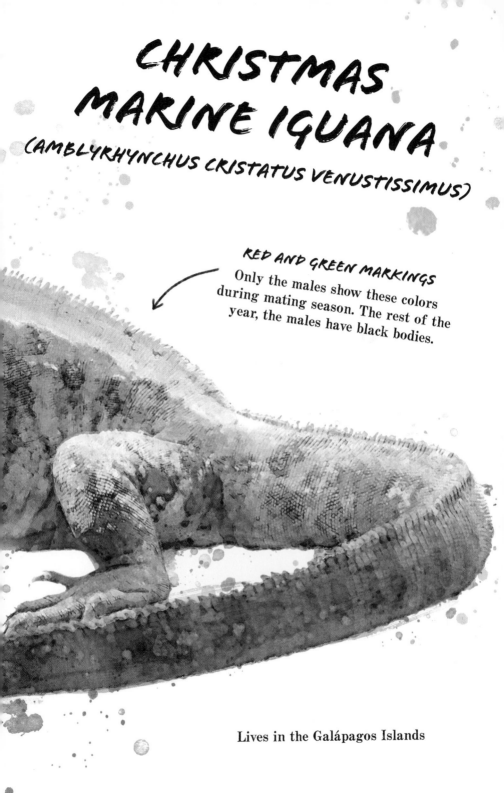

RED AND GREEN MARKINGS
Only the males show these colors during mating season. The rest of the year, the males have black bodies.

Lives in the Galápagos Islands

MALES 4–5 FEET LONG (1.2–1.5 METERS);
FEMALES 2–3 FEET LONG (0.6–0.9 METER)

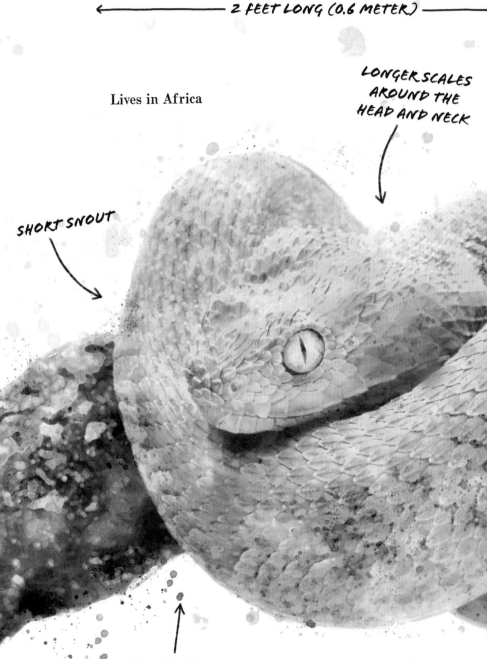

Lives in Africa

LONGER SCALES AROUND THE HEAD AND NECK

SHORT SNOUT

HINGED FANGS

Vipers are a family of venomous snakes most well-known for their long, pointed fangs. When the snake isn't using them, the fangs fold up and back into its mouth, almost disappearing.

RAISED, POINTED SCALES

These scales give the rain forest-dwelling bush viper a bristly, hairy appearance.

AFRICAN HAIRY BUSH VIPER

(ATHERIS HISPIDA)

LONG, HORNLIKE
SPINES ON HEAD AND
DOWN THE BACK

DARK BODY WITH
GREEN MARKINGS

STRONG LEGS

The horned tree agamid is
arboreal (tree dwelling). Its
coloring helps it blend into the
forests of Phuket's mountainous
region. It lives just in that small
region of Thailand, and it was
only discovered a few years ago.

Lives in Thailand

TEETH ON OUTER RIDGE OF MOUTH

The horned tree agamid eats insects and the occasional fish. It uses a "sit-and-wait" hunting style, sitting very still while waiting to pounce on prey.

LARGE SKIN FOLD UNDER NECK

PHUKET HORNED TREE AGAMID

(ACANTHOSAURA PHUKETENSIS)

WIDE RIB CAGE

The wide rib cage supports the membrane flaps. The flying dragon flattens its body as it glides to help it stay in the air.

MEMBRANE FLAPS

The flaps have a circular shape that lets the flying dragon glide through the air. The movement helps it get from one tree to another and can help it quickly escape predators.

Lives in Southeast Asia

GREEN AND BROWN COLORING

Its coloring, along with the shape of the flaps, acts as camouflage. It looks like a leaf falling through the air when it glides.

BORNEO FLYING DRAGON

(DRACO CORNUTUS)

Lives in the southeastern
United States

GRAY, BROWN, OR BLACK COLORING

The color helps camouflage it, since the alligator snapping turtle spends most of its time in the water. When it hunts, it stays motionless and nearly invisible under the water for more than 40 minutes, only coming up to the surface for air.

TALL RIDGES ON SHELL

WEIGHS NEARLY 200 POUNDS (91 KILOGRAMS)

The alligator snapping turtle is the largest freshwater turtle. It lives in large bodies of deep water, like rivers, lakes, or swamps.

← ——————— 2.5–3 FEET LONG (0.76–0.9 METER) —

ALLIGATOR SNAPPING TURTLE

(MACROCHELYS TEMMINCKII)

EYES ON SIDE OF HEAD

POINTED SNOUT

PINK TONGUE

The tongue looks like a worm and attracts fish like a lure. Once a fish gets close enough, the turtle snaps its jaws shut, trapping the fish and often swallowing it whole. It also eats mollusks, insects, and other small reptiles.

LARGE, POWERFUL JAWS

GIANT GIRDLED LIZARD

(SMAUG GIGANTEUS)

Lives in South Africa

LONG NAILS

The girdled lizard lives in burrows it digs. It's very territorial, and it rarely strays far from its home.

BODY COVERED WITH POINTED, SPINY SCALES

The scales work as a type of armor to protect the girdled lizard from predators. They also help it to regulate its temperature. The girdled lizard is sometimes called a sungazer lizard because it likes to rest staring up toward the sun.

ARMORED TAIL, COVERED IN THICK, LARGE, SPINY SCALES

If it feels threatened, it'll sometimes go partially into the burrow, leaving its tail exposed and swinging it around to deter intruders.

— 1–1.5 FEET LONG (0.3–0.45 METER) —→

SMOOTH-FRONTED CAIMAN

(PALEOSUCHUS TRIGONATUS)

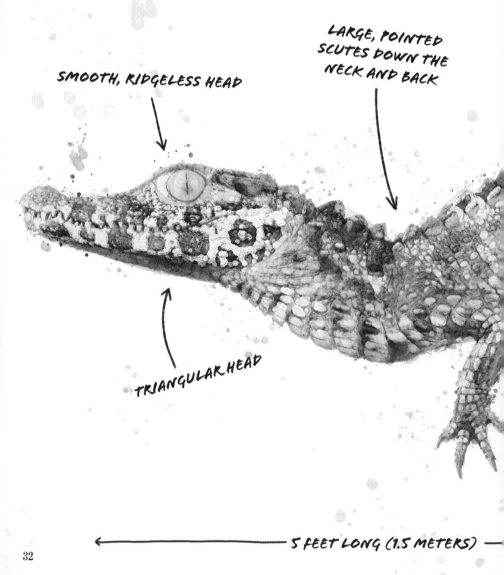

SMOOTH, RIDGELESS HEAD

LARGE, POINTED SCUTES DOWN THE NECK AND BACK

TRIANGULAR HEAD

5 FEET LONG (1.5 METERS)

DARK-GRAY BODY

The caiman hunts both in the water and on land. It eats fish, reptiles, and aquatic insects. Adult caimans usually move to the forest, looking for bigger prey like porcupines and pacas.

WEIGHS 80 POUNDS (36 KILOGRAMS)

BROAD-BASED, SHORT TAIL

The smooth-fronted caiman has side-facing scutes on its tail. Scutes are bony, armor-like plates. The caiman's tail is so heavily armored that it's inflexible.

PINOCCHIO LIZARD

(ANOLIS PROBOSCIS)

SMALL BODY

GREEN COLOR

The Pinocchio lizard was first described in 1956, but then nobody spotted another one for about 40 years. It was rediscovered in 2005 by bird-watchers. The green color helps it to camouflage with the trees.

9–11 INCHES LONG (22.86–28 CENTIMETERS)

Lives in Ecuador

LONG, PROTRUDING SNOUT

At the end of the snout is an appendage called a proboscis that looks like a horn. Only the males have the characteristic horn. Scientists aren't quite sure why they have it, but even male hatchlings have a small horn.

SHORT LIMBS

The Pinocchio lizard moves very, very slowly, making it difficult to see.

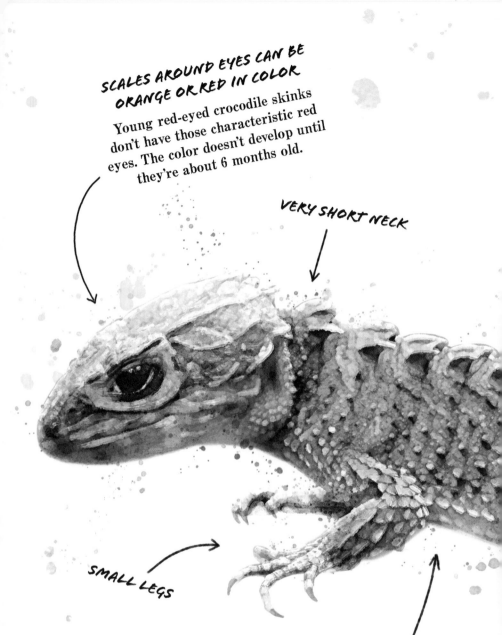

SCALES AROUND EYES CAN BE ORANGE OR RED IN COLOR

Young red-eyed crocodile skinks don't have those characteristic red eyes. The color doesn't develop until they're about 6 months old.

VERY SHORT NECK

SMALL LEGS

BROWN OR GRAY BODY

The forest-dwelling crocodile skink makes nests under forest debris and soil. It likes to be near water and is sometimes found on coconut plantations.

RED-EYED CROCODILE SKINK

(TRIBOLONOTUS GRACILIS)

Lives in Papua New Guinea
and the Admiralty Islands

ROW OF CROCODILE-LIKE
SCALES DOWN THE BACK

6-8 INCHES LONG
(15.2-20.3 CENTIMETERS)

RATTLE TAIL

The diamondback rattlesnake makes noise by rapidly moving its rattle-like tail tip. The rattle portion itself is made up of loosely attached, hollow segments. When it senses danger, it makes the rattling noise to scare away the threat. But when it's hunting prey and doesn't want to be heard, the rattlesnake can stay silent.

Lives in the southeastern United States

VENOMOUS FANGS THAT FOLD BACK WHEN NOT IN USE

It hunts small rodents and birds as well as some larger prey like rabbits. It will attack if it feels threatened, and the venom is strong enough to kill a person if it's left untreated.

EASTERN DIAMONDBACK RATTLESNAKE

(CROTALUS ADAMANTEUS)

PATTERN OF DIAMOND SHAPES DOWN THE BACK WITH YELLOW OR TAN SCALES

The beautiful markings can actually be what kills them—people hunt the diamondbacks for their prized skin.

OLIVE, BROWN, OR BLACK COLORING

4–6 FEET LONG (1.2–1.8 METERS)

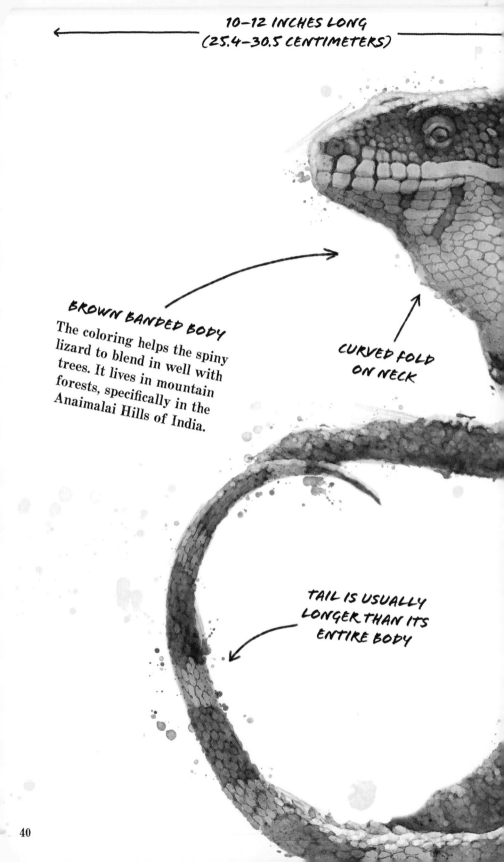

BROWN BANDED BODY
The coloring helps the spiny lizard to blend in well with trees. It lives in mountain forests, specifically in the Anaimalai Hills of India.

CURVED FOLD ON NECK

TAIL IS USUALLY LONGER THAN ITS ENTIRE BODY

ANAIMALAI SPINY LIZARD
(SALEA ANAMALLAYANA)

Lives in India

TALL, POINTED
SPINES ALONG
THE BACK

LONG HIND LEGS

The spiny lizard is slow
moving. It doesn't run
when threatened. Instead,
it freezes and tries to
avoid being noticed.

USAMBARA THREE-HORNED CHAMELEON

(TRIOCEROS DEREMENSIS)

THREE LARGE HORNS ON FACE

LONG TONGUE

Chameleons have a unique feeding method, shooting out their incredibly long tongues to catch insects out of the air and pull them in.

JOINED EYELIDS

The pupil only sees out of a small hole in between the upper and lower eyelids, and the eyes can move independently of each other, meaning they can look in different directions at the same time.

Lives in Tanzania

LONG, CURLING TAIL

The tail is prehensile, which means it can grasp onto things. The tail helps so much when the chameleon is climbing trees that it's jokingly called a fifth limb.

SHARP CLAW
ON EACH TOE

12–16 INCHES LONG
(30.5–40.6 CENTIMETERS)

INDIAN NARROW-HEADED SOFTSHELL TURTLE

(CHITRA INDICA)

Lives in South Asia

SOFT SHELL

The shell is leathery and flexible, which makes it easy for the Indian narrow-headed softshell turtle to bury under sand or mud.

WEBBED FEET

← 2–3 FEET LONG (0.6–0.9 METER) →